HISTORY OF BRITAIN

MEDIEVAL BRITAIN

1066 to 1485

Revised and updated

Brenda Williams

Heinemann
LIBRARY

www.heinemann.co.uk/library
Visit our website to find out more information about Heinemann Library books.

To order:
☎ Phone 44 (0) 1865 8881
🖷 Send a fax to 44 (0) 186
💻 Visit the Heinemann Bookshop
   catalogue and order or

First published in Great Britain by Heinemann Library,
Halley Court, Jordan Hill, Oxford OX2 8EJ, part of
Harcourt Education.
Heinemann is a registered trademark of Harcourt
Education Ltd.

© Harcourt Education Ltd 1994, 2006
The moral right of the proprietor has been asserted.

Editorial: Lionel Bender and Richard Woodham
Design: Ben White and Michelle Lisseter
Picture Research: Jennie Karrach and Mica Brancic
Production: Helen McCreath

Originated by RMW
Printed and bound in China by WKT Company Limited

10 digit ISBN 0 431 10811 0
13 digit ISBN 978 0 431 10811 7
10 09 08 07 06
10 9 8 7 6 5 4 3 2 1

British Library Cataloguing in Publication Data
Williams, Brenda
Medieval Britain. - 2nd ed. - (History of Britain)
941'.02
A full catalogue record for this book is available from the
British Library.

Acknowledgements
The publishers would like to thank the following for
permission to reproduce photographs:
Page 7 (top): Michael Holford; 7 (bottom): Aerofilms
Limited; Page 9 (left): Public Record Office; Page 9
(right): Cambridge University Collection/British Crown
Copyright/MOD; Reproduced with the permission of
Controller of HMSO; Page 11 (top): The British
Library/MS 42130 f171; Page 11 (bottom): The British
Library/MS 42130 f193; Page 12: Michael Holford; Page
13: The British Library/Royal MS 14C VII f8v; Page 14:
Bodleian Library, Oxford/BODL 264 fol 112R left; Page 15:
The British Library/Hari MS 326 f113; Page 17 (left):
Corpus Christi College, Cambridge/MS 16 f155v; Page 17
(right): Canterbury Heritage Museums; Page 18:
Canterbury Heritage Museums; Page 19 (top): The British
Library/Cotton MS Claudius BII f341; Page 19 (bottom):
The British Library/Add 28,681 f9; Page 20: The British
Library/Sloane MS 2435 f44v; Page 21: Aerofilms; Page
22: The British Library/Cotton MS Augustus II.106; Page
22 (top): The British Library/Articles of the Barons
MS4838, reverse; Page 23: Wriothesley manuscript
113/The Royal Collection 1994 Her Majesty the Queen;
Page 24: Michael Holford; Page 25: Corpus Christi
College, Cambridge/MS16 f132r; Page 26: Werner
Forman Archive/Westminster Abbey; Page 27: The
British Library/Cotton Nero D.VI, f61v; Page 28: The
British Library/MS 17012 f6; Page 29: Michael Holford;
Page 30 (top): Museum of London; Page 30 (bottom):
Jean Williamson/Mick Sharp; Page 32 (top): Michael
Holford; Page 32 (bottom): Sonia Halliday and Laura
Lushington; Page 33: The British Library/Royal 15EII f265;
Page 34: The Bodleian Library, Oxford MS BODL 264,
fol181v; Page 35: Sonia Halliday Photographs; Page 36
(top): Courtesy of the Trustees of the British Museum
0.1.20 f262R; Page 36 (bottom): Bibliotheek Albert I,
Brussels; Page 39 (top): The British Library/Royal MS 18E
I 175; Page 39 (bottom): Mick Sharp; Page 40:
Department of the Environment, Crown Copyright; Page
41: The British Library/ Royal MS 20 C VII f41v; Page 42:
The National Portrait Gallery; Page 43: Mick Sharp.

Illustrations by John James: 6/7, 8/9, 14/15, 18/19, 22/23,
30/31, 32/33, 42/43; James Field: 10/11, 12/13, 16/17, 24/25,
26/27, 34/35, 38/39; Bill Donohoe: 20/21; Mark Bergin
28/29, 36/37, 40/41; Hayward Art: page 9.

Cover photograph of Gilbert de Clare, 3rd Earl of
Gloucester (1243–95), after a stained glass window of
c.1340 in Tewkesbury Abbey Church (litho) by Shaw,
Henry (1800–73), reproduced with permission of
Bridgeman.

The publishers would like to thank Andrew Langley for
his assistance in the preparation of this book.

Every effort has been made to contact copyright holders
of any material reproduced in this book.
Any omissions will be rectified in subsequent printings if
notice is given to the publishers.

The paper used to print this book comes from
sustainable resources.

CONTENTS

*Unfamiliar words are explained in the **glossary** on page 46*

ABOUT THIS BOOK

This book considers the Modern period chronologically, meaning that events are described in the order in which they happened, from 1901 to the present day. Some of the double-page articles deal with a particular part of modern history. Those that deal with aspects of everyday life, such as trade, houses, and pastimes, are more general and cover a broader timescale. The small illustrations at the top of the left-hand pages show, in chronological order, major scientific developments, discoveries, and inventions of modern times in Britain.

Unfamiliar words are explained in the glossary on page 46.

▼ **This map** shows the location of places mentioned in the text. Some are major cities, towns, or the sites of famous buildings or events.

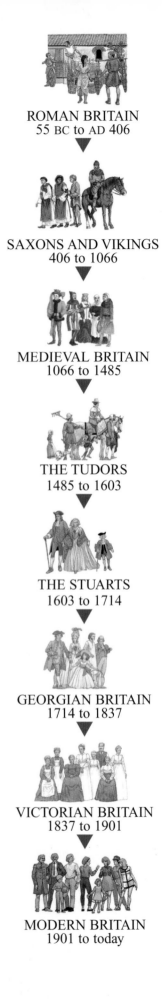

ROMAN BRITAIN
55 BC to AD 406

SAXONS AND VIKINGS
406 to 1066

MEDIEVAL BRITAIN
1066 to 1485

THE TUDORS
1485 to 1603

THE STUARTS
1603 to 1714

GEORGIAN BRITAIN
1714 to 1837

VICTORIAN BRITAIN
1837 to 1901

MODERN BRITAIN
1901 to today

INTRODUCTION

In 1066, Saxon England was conquered by invaders from Normandy in France. The effects of the Norman settlement were also felt in Wales, Scotland, and Ireland.

Most people in medieval Britain were farmers who did not own the land they farmed. They worked on land held by a nobleman. The nobles in turn were bound by duty and loyalty to the king. Medieval kings had power over everyone, but even they accepted the authority of the Christian Church, whose head was the Pope in Rome. The Church, through its monasteries, was the centre of learning, art, and scholarship.

In England, the Normans made French, not English, the language of law and government. Few people could read or write, except monks. But from the 1100s, monks and government clerks copied out more and more written laws, treaties, land deeds, household accounts, and other documents which give historians a detailed view of everyday life. Much of what we know of Norman England comes from the unique land survey ordered by William I, called the Domesday Book. There are chronicles, or histories, written by monks and scholars; family records, such as the Paston Letters written in the 1400s; and the writings of poets such as Gower, Langland, and Chaucer, who is most famous for his *Canterbury Tales* (written about 1386 to 1400). Tomb-sculptures, paintings, and carvings in wood and stone show us what people looked like then. The most powerful kings of medieval Britain were the kings of England. They conquered Wales, fought for Scotland, raided Ireland, and for many years battled for the throne of France. This book tells the story of their times from the Norman Conquest to the first of the Tudors.

THE NORMANS CONQUER

In September 1066, a fleet sailed from France to Britain with the army of Duke William of Normandy. He had come to claim the English crown. The Normans landed in Sussex and the English marched to meet them. Saxon rule of England ended with the death in battle of Harold, the last Saxon king.

William waited at Hastings for the English nobles to come and hail him as their new king. When they did not, he marched his army towards London, ravaging the country as he went. The Norman duke knew how to make people fear and obey him. Soon most of the English leaders agreed that the kingdom was his by right of conquest. He was crowned in Westminster Abbey on Christmas Day 1066.

▽ **An early-Norman motte and bailey castle** could be built in 2 weeks.
● The motte was an earth mound, with a wooden tower on top.
● Ox-hides soaked in water protected the walls from fire when attacked.
● Inside lived the baron, his family and servants.
● At the foot of the mound was the bailey. In this enclosure were stables, barracks for soldiers, store-houses and a kitchen.

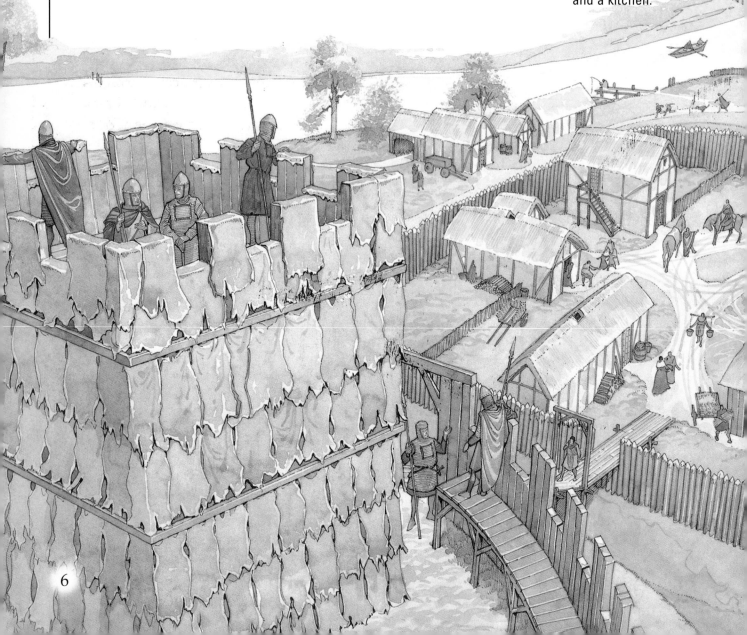

△ **Normans build a castle at Hastings** – from the Bayeux Tapestry that tells the story of the Conquest.

William had to show he was master of England and its people. He had only a small army with which to control the country. So he and his nobles, called barons, built castles to guard roads, rivers, and towns. From these wooden forts, the Normans ruled the land. Cavalry patrols rode out to keep order.

William controlled south and central England, but faced revolts in the west and north. After an uprising in 1069, William burned large areas of rebel lands in the north. Among the few English to fight on was Hereward the Wake, in Lincolnshire. The Scots king Malcolm Canmore raided England too, but later swore loyalty to William.

At first, William let English nobles keep most of their lands. But soon he gave the lands to his Norman followers. After 1071 the king spent much of his time in Normandy and he needed loyal barons in England to defend his throne and their new lands. Twenty years after the Conquest, only two English nobles still held lands of importance.

◁ **Around the castle was a village.** This is Pevensey Castle and village, Sussex, today. The Normans used stone to build a rectangular tower (top left) and a wall with round towers within the walls of a Roman fort.
● Some castles were surrounded by a ditch.
● In the village of thatched houses and farms lived the English.
● By 1100, the Normans had built at least 500 castles in England.

ENGLAND AT DOMESDAY

William I spent Christmas at Gloucester in 1085, talking with his council "about this land, how it was peopled, and with what sort of men". Then he sent officials to travel around England, to collect details of every village for the great survey called Domesday.

Nobody could argue with the Domesday (Day of Judgement) Book's records on who held what land. All land in England was the king's. The barons held their lands from him, and fought for him in return. The barons also supplied the king with trained soldiers called knights, who held land from the barons.

Ordinary people held their small plots of land from a lord – a baron or knight, a bishop, or abbot of the Church, or even from the king. In return they worked on the lord's land, gave him some of their crops, eggs and meat, paid him money, and fought for him when ordered.

▷ **A typical village of the Domesday period.** In the centre of the village was the church, crossroads, and often the lord's manor house. Around these were peasants' houses (crofts) with small gardens (tofts).

▷ **In little more than a year, the Domesday officers** visited villages across England to find who held what land, what the land was worth and what animals the land-holder owned.
● Details were collected county by county.
● Winchester, London, and the most northerly counties have no record.
● People gave details on oath, based on the day of the survey and the "day when (Saxon) King Edward (the Confessor) was alive and dead" (that is, 1066).

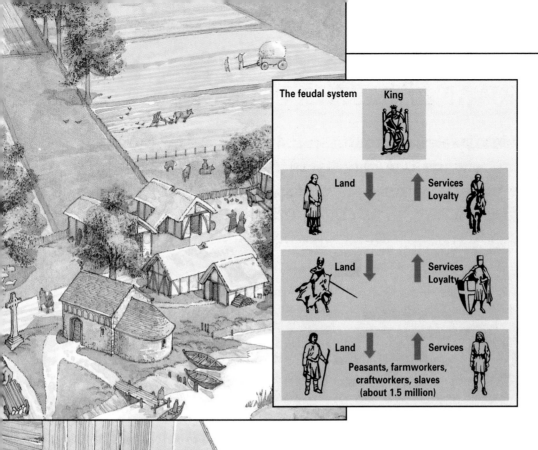

The feudal system

King

Land → ← Services Loyalty

Land → ← Services Loyalty

Land → ← Services

Peasants, farmworkers, craftworkers, slaves (about 1.5 million)

◁ **In Norman England people held land from a lord in return for service.** This is called feudalism.

● The king let out lands (fiefs) to barons and the Church, who let lands in turn to knights. Knights let lands to peasants.

● By doing homage, or swearing loyalty to his lord, a man became a vassal. In return, he got protection and justice.

● Peasants served their lord by farming the land.

● Slaves held no land, but slavery soon died out.

◁ **Domesday Book** gives a unique account of life in England between 1066 and 1088. It names some 13,000 settlements, and shows that most people lived in country villages. The majority were villeins (villagers) with land in the village fields. Next in number were "cottars" or "bordars", with just a cottage or garden. A few people were poor and landless slaves.

△ **The layout of strip fields of crops** around a village much as it was in the Middle Ages can be seen clearly from the air at Laxton in Nottinghamshire. Surrounding meadows were used as grazing land for sheep and cattle, and woodland provided timber for buildings.

William's inquiry was so thorough that "there was not... even one ox, nor one cow, nor one pig which escaped notice", said a chronicler. A typical entry in the survey reads: "In Wallington, Fulco holds of Gilbert 3 hides and 40 acres of land. There is land for five ploughs... There is pasture for beasts and wood for hedges... Altogether it is worth 50s (50 shillings). When he received it, 30s. At the time of King Edward, 100s (£5)".

England rapidly became Norman. Its nobles and bishops had Norman names, and new buildings were Norman in style. People still spoke English, but Church or government officials spoke French and wrote in Latin.

MANORS AND PEASANTS

By 1100 there were about 5,000 barons and knights living in England's castles and great houses. Most other people, over a million of them, were peasants, farm workers or craftsmen. They lived in farming communities that the Domesday Book calls manors.

The lord of the manor lived on his estate in his manor house. Some distance away were the small houses and fields of his peasant vassals. Some peasants paid rent for land and at times worked for their lord. Others had to work for part of each week on the lord's land and give him some of their produce. Yet more of their crops, eggs, and meat (a tenth, or tithe) had to be given to the Church. Such peasants had to stay on the manor where they were born. Everything they had – money, cattle, tools – belonged in law to their lord. They paid for their corn to be ground at the lord's mill and to take wood from the forest.

All vassals had to give a lord "reliefs" (money, food, or goods) at certain times. For example, when a peasant died, his son had to give the lord his best animal and the priest his second best. He paid a fine if a daughter left the village after marrying, or if a son left to become a monk.

△ **Peasants kept their animals** fenced-off in their houses, as shown above. Each manor produced all its own food.
● The village had two or three large fields divided into narrow strips.
● Each peasant had strips in different parts of the field, so each shared good and poor land.
● Fields lay fallow (had nothing grown on them) every other year.
● People grew rye, oats, peas, and barley as crops.

△ **A young peasant's day began at sunrise.** He had probably slept on a bed of straw, and had eaten no breakfast.

△ **He also helped his father plough the fields** and his mother to sow seeds, tend the garden, or gather firewood.

He watched over grazing sheep or cattle and drove birds from newly-sown fields by shaking a rattle.

△ **Dinner was eaten** at mid-morning. There might be pottage, a vegetable stew, and bread. Ale was drunk from a leather mug.

◁ **Peasants wore warm clothes.** Women wore a long woollen gown and men a woollen shirt. Both might have a linen shirt for underwear. Hoods or scarves, and woollen stockings, were worn in winter. Shoes were made of leather or wood.

Work on the manor was planned by the reeve, who was chosen as the peasants' spokesman. His orders came from the lord's bailiff, who took orders from the lord's steward. The bailiff also hired skilled workers, such as carpenters, millers, and smiths. Manors varied in different parts of the country, and a great noble might own a number of manors in many places. Some manors were made up of bits of land from several villages.

△ **A sheep's ears were marked** and its fleece cut off with shears. Women spun the fleece into wool fibres, as shown far right.

△ **Supper was eaten** around 4:00 p.m.. Bread and eggs was the usual meal. When darkness fell, the family went to bed.

△ **In spring, seed was sown on soil broken up by the harrow** (top manuscript illustration). Summer was haymaking and harvest time. Corn was cut with sickles. Autumn was the season for ploughing. Peasants shared the heavy plough and the oxen that pulled it.

THE LORD'S CASTLE

"They filled the land full of castles and... filled them with devils and evil men", said a chronicler in 1137. The castle was the centre of local power. It was a law court and a government office, where the baron's officials kept the manor records. Villagers paid taxes and fines at the castle. It was also the local prison.

▷ **Stone castles** like this one built in the 1120s at Rochester, Kent, gradually replaced early wooden forts. The keep, or central tower, was still the strongest point. Around it were built thick defensive walls, as here. A castle was weakest at the gate. A gatehouse, or barbican, was built to protect it. Castles might have a flooded ditch, or moat, with a drawbridge across it. A portcullis – a huge iron gate – could also be let down to bar the way in.

The great hall was the castle's living room. Here everybody ate and some people slept, either on benches or on dried reeds spread over the floor. Early castles had a log fire in the middle of the hall. There were no chimneys and the room grew very smoky. Later castles had fireplaces. Walls might be plastered, painted, or hung with tapestries.

Some barons' families also had a private room called a solar, where they could rest by day and sleep at night. It was either an area screened off in the great hall or a room at the top of the keep.

▷ **The local lord settles a dispute in the main hall of the castle keep.** Castles were dark and cold, with open arches for windows, and narrow slits through which soldiers could fire arrows. There was no glass, but shutters to close out the weather. The floors were wooden. Stone stairs wound round the castle walls. Toilets were in wall spaces built out over the moat and emptied straight into it.

◁ **The four Norman kings of England were** (top left to bottom right):

● William I (1066–1087). After William's death, his eldest son, Robert, ruled Normandy; his second son, William, ruled England.

● William II (1087–1100) was a good soldier who quarrelled with the Church. He was killed by an arrow while hunting.

● Henry I (1100–1135), William I's third son, beat his brother Robert in battle to gain Normandy. Henry's only son was drowned and England's next king was his nephew:

● Stephen (1135–1154). He fought Henry's daughter, Matilda, in a civil war. When Stephen died, Matilda's son Henry Plantagenet became king.

Most castles had a chapel, or small church for prayer. The kitchen, store-room for food and drink, and the brewery, where beer was made, were under the great hall or in the bailey.

Within the great hall, the manor court was held. Here the baron judged criminals and disputes about land. The castle prison was in the keep, where the weapons and armour were also held.

Barons needed the king's permission to build a castle. In busy towns, houses were sometimes pulled down to make way for the new building. Lincoln lost 166 houses in this way. The king did not want his barons to grow too powerful, but he was pleased for them to build castles on the Welsh border and in the north, to defend his kingdom's frontiers.

LORDS AND LADIES

Norman barons were fighting men. When not at war, they enjoyed sports that kept them in training for battle. They hunted on horseback with bows and spears. They held mock battles called tournaments, or jousted with lances. Hunting also provided meat for the castle household.

After a successful hunt there was feasting in the great hall. The baron's family sat with their guests on a raised platform at one end of the room. They watched the meat roasting on a spit over the fire. Then trumpets or a gong sounded for the meal to begin. Dishes at a special feast might include swan, heron, peacock or gulls, with venison (deer meat) and wild boar from the hunt. Soldiers and servants of the household had bread and salted meat, with ale to drink. The baron drank wine and ate with a spoon and knife, not with his fingers. Minstrels played and sang while the company feasted.

A squire waited on his lord at table. He was a noble's son, sent to the castle as a boy of 7 years old to be trained. At first he was a page, and learned to fight, to act like a lord, and perhaps to read and write. At 15 he became a squire and took part in battle. At 20 he was ready for knighthood.

△ **Normans loved hunting.** This scene shows a lord returning from a stag hunt and telling his lady of his kill. William I "loved the stag, as dearly as though he had been their father", noted a chronicler. Norman kings set up forests as private hunting parks. One included the entire county of Essex! A poacher who stole any animal from a royal forest risked having a hand cut off.

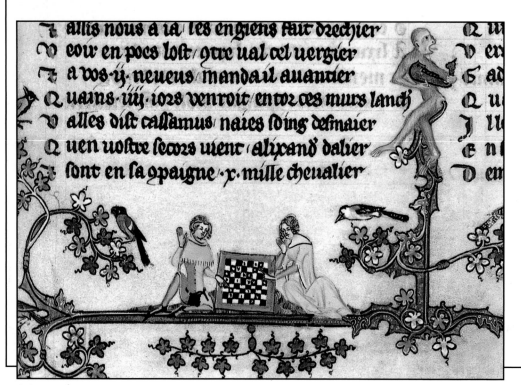

◁ **A medieval manuscript illustration** showing a lady and a knight playing chess together in a manor garden. A monkey is shown as a minstrel.

▷ **Lords and ladies enjoyed hawking,** or falconry, both for fresh meat and for sport. Hawks were trained to catch other birds, mice, and hares. When not flying, the hawks were fitted with a hood to calm them. The falconer wore a glove to protect him from the bird's claws and beak.

△ **Tournaments were mock battles** between two groups of armoured knights on horseback. The fight took place over a wide area and people who came to watch often joined in! Deaths were frequent. Jousts were contests between two mounted knights charging one another with lances.

The baron's lady taught her own young children as well as older girls from nearby great houses. She managed a large staff of servants but could do all the household tasks herself. Many women ran both the castle and the estate when the baron was at war or at the king's court. All women in the Middle Ages could spin, weave, sew, and make clothes. They enjoyed dancing and singing. Noblewomen played games such as chess. They fished and went hawking. Most marriages were arranged by parents. Girls were often promised to husbands, or were even married, while still children.

THE KING'S LAW

Stephen, the last Norman king of England, died in 1154. Weak government during the civil war against Matilda had let barons grow lawless. They built castles without permission, fought each other, and seized lands from weaker men. Crime flourished. The new king, Henry II, began to regain royal control.

▷ **Henry II, his officials, soldiers, and followers ride back to Orford Castle** in Suffolk, where the king is in judgement at one of his courts. In the castle bailey, criminals are being hanged on the gallows or put in the stocks.

Henry gained lands by war and cunning, forcing Malcolm IV of Scotland to give up border regions to England in 1157. Henry led armies to Wales, and the Welsh princes recognized him as overlord. In 1171 he went to Ireland, took it under his rule, and made his son John, Lord of Ireland.

But Henry quarrelled with his wife, Eleanor, who then helped their sons to revolt and turn against him.

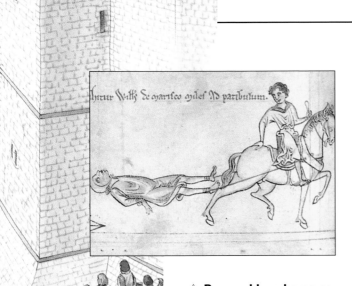

▷ **The seal of the monks at Canterbury.** The personal seal of a lord, bishop, or king gave a grant, or charter, its authority. More and more legal documents were made from the 12th century onwards. By Edward III's reign, even serfs had a seal.

△ **Dragged by a horse** as punishment for a crime. Henry's law reforms (changes) meant that all free men could seek justice at the local court or, if that failed, at a king's court. Judges travelled from one king's court to the next. From 1180 there was a permanent royal court at Westminster.

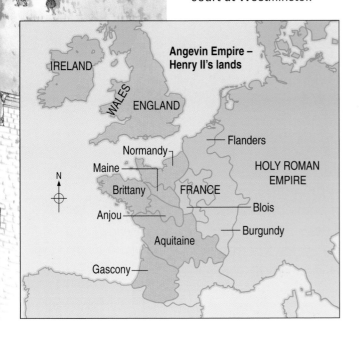

Angevin Empire – Henry II's lands

IRELAND

WALES

ENGLAND

Flanders

Normandy

Maine

HOLY ROMAN EMPIRE

N

Brittany

FRANCE

Anjou

Blois

Aquitaine

Burgundy

Gascony

△ **Henry's lands are often called the Angevin Empire,** after the region of Anjou in France. Henry became Count of Anjou when his father died in 1151. Through his mother, Matilda, he gained Normandy in 1150 and England in 1154. Henry gained Aquitaine in France through his marriage to Eleanor in 1152.

Henry II had great energy. It was said that he never sat down but was always on the move, travelling round his lands in England and France. Henry wanted his kingdom governed as well as in the days of his grandfather, Henry I.

First he dealt with the barons. He destroyed castles they had built without royal permission and set out to return stolen land to its rightful holders. Most disputes about land-holding were heard in the barons' courts. They could be settled by trial by battle, where the strongest fighter won. Henry insisted that land disputes be brought to one of the king's courts, where the local sheriff called a jury to hear cases. This was a more just, or fairer, way of deciding rights and wrongs.

Suspected criminals were rounded up, too. A jury of 12 men from each hundred (an area of local government) and four from each town reported local law-breakers to the sheriff or royal justice. The suspects were then put to "trial by ordeal". Some had to carry a red-hot iron bar for three paces, or pull out a stone from boiling water. Those whose skin blistered from burns were guilty and could be hanged, put in prison or the stocks, be blinded, or maimed.

CHURCH AND KING

The most powerful man in England after the king was the Archbishop of Canterbury, leader of the Church. The king could choose the Archbishop, but the Church had its own laws and courts and its ruler was the Pope in Rome. All England had to obey the Pope, even the king.

Pilgrim's badge, Canterbury.

The Pope was the leader of the Christian world. Most people in Europe were Christians and believed that through the Pope, God told them what to do. In 1095 the Pope called on Christians to free the holy places of Palestine, where Jesus had lived. These parts of the Middle East, including the city of Jerusalem, were under Muslim control and had been closed to Christian pilgrims. Jerusalem was a holy city to Muslims as well as to Christians. The wars called the Crusades (wars of the cross) went on for the next 200 years. Kings, barons, knights and thousands of ordinary people set out from Europe to seek forgiveness for their sins by fighting the Muslims in Palestine.

But kings did not always obey the Pope. During the unrest of the 1150s, the Church had seized some powers from the monarchy. Now Henry II wanted those powers back.

△ **Pilgrims visited shrines** where saints' bodies or their remains were kept.
● They prayed for healing, or for their sins to be pardoned.
● Pilgrims to St Thomas' shrine at Canterbury (above) could buy bottles of what was said to be the saint's blood to use for healing.
● Each shrine had its own symbol (top). Jerusalem sold a palm leaf badge to pilgrims.

William I's archbishop, Lanfranc, had set up Church courts. He also reformed the English Church in line with the Pope's rules against married priests and against priests buying important Church jobs.

● The Normans built great cathedrals, such as Durham, Norwich, and Winchester.

● Bishops and other Church leaders were better educated than kings and barons.

◁ **The murder of Archbishop Becket** in Canterbury Cathedral in 1170.

△ **Medieval map of the Christian world.** Pilgrims to Jerusalem (at the centre of the map) faced attack from bandits, and wild animals such as lions and panthers. Pilgrims in Europe travelled far to visit holy places. Canterbury and Durham, which kept St Cuthbert's relics, were the chief centres for pilgrims in England.

Henry needed an Archbishop of Canterbury who would do what he told him. In 1162 he chose his trusted advisor, Thomas Becket. But Becket quickly became a fierce defender of the Church's rights. Henry saw Becket as a traitor and in anger is said to have exclaimed, "Will no one rid me of this turbulent priest?" Four knights, supposedly acting on Henry's behalf, killed Becket in Canterbury Cathedral.

The murder shocked Christians throughout Europe. Before long, there were reports of miracles at Becket's tomb, and Canterbury became a shrine (a special holy place) to which pilgrims flocked for healing. The Pope made Becket a saint. Henry himself made a pilgrimage to Canterbury. He walked barefoot through the town and, at his request, was flogged by bishops and monks as a punishment.

MONKS AND MONASTERIES

The number of monks and nuns in England had grown from about 1,000 in 1066 to about 13,000 by 1215. On feast days, the monks of Rievaulx Abbey in Yorkshire were "unable to move forward because of the multitude clustered together." So says a life of St Ailred, abbot of Rievaulx from 1146.

▷ **A monk's day was one of work and prayer.**
● 12:00 a.m: a bell woke him for the first services (right). He went back to bed at about 1:30 a.m.
● 7:00 a.m: the day began.
● 11:30 a.m: Dinner, followed by exercise and 5 hours' work.
● After supper: monks read or talked before bed at 7:30 to 8:30 p.m.

Monks and nuns spent their lives in prayer and work for God. They followed the Rule of St Benedict, set down around 535 to 540. This stated that a monk must be poor, unmarried and obedient. In the 11th century new groups, or orders, of monks had been formed and built their own monasteries. Among them was the Cistercian order, originally from France.

Monasteries became centres of a revival of learning. They founded hospitals and cathedral schools, and produced scholars who started universities at Oxford (before 1209) and Cambridge (between 1209 and 1214). In 1221 Dominican friars came to England from Spain. They were wandering preachers who at first lived by begging. Then came Franciscan friars from Italy.

Monks went to these services each day: Matins at midnight, Lauds, Prime, Terce, Sext at noon, Nones, Vespers and Compline.

△ **Monks ate in the refectory.** One monk read aloud during the simple meal (left). A monk wore a long robe (above).

▽ **The cellarer** was a monk who kept the monastery keys and sampled the wine. Monks were often accused of drinking far too much wine.

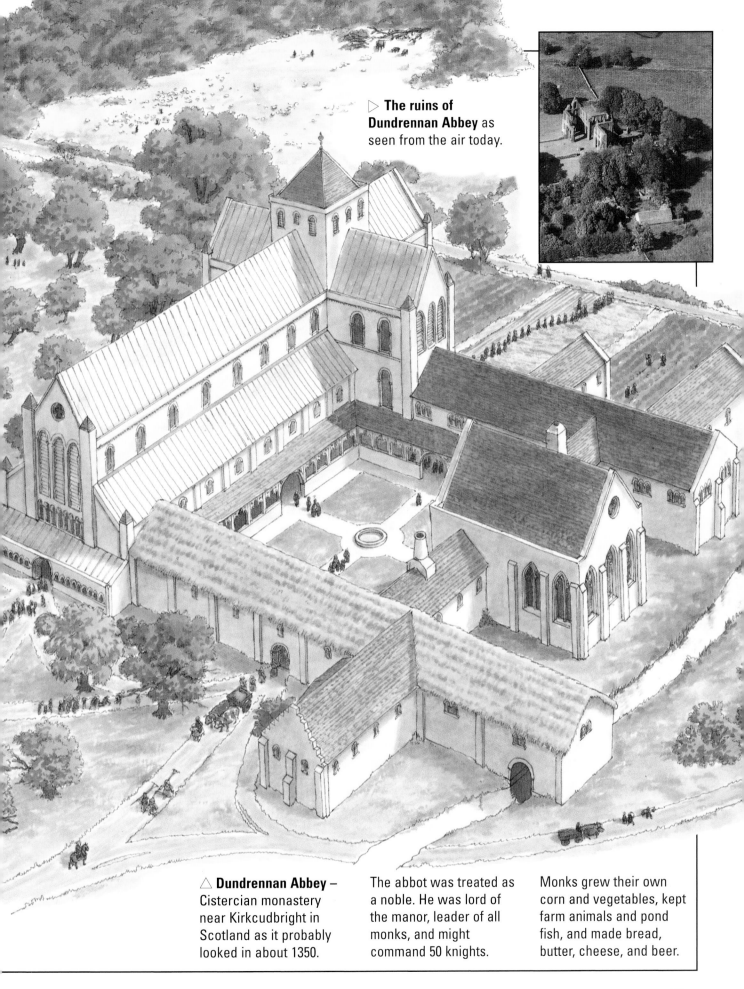

▷ **The ruins of Dundrennan Abbey** as seen from the air today.

△ **Dundrennan Abbey** – Cistercian monastery near Kirkcudbright in Scotland as it probably looked in about 1350.

The abbot was treated as a noble. He was lord of the manor, leader of all monks, and might command 50 knights.

Monks grew their own corn and vegetables, kept farm animals and pond fish, and made bread, butter, cheese, and beer.

CHANGES IN GOVERNMENT

Henry II died in 1189. His son, Richard I, spent just six months of his 10-year reign in England. While he was away fighting wars, barons, and churchmen governed for him. Their struggle to play a greater part in government led to civil war in later reigns.

▷ **King John's seal on Magna Carta**

▷ **The Magna Carta, or Great Charter, was set before King John at Runnymede, Surrey, in June 1215.** The charter controlled royal power by forcing the king to ask for the barons' agreement in such matters as new taxes. Of the 63 articles, or terms, most made the king promise to uphold the rights of the Church and barons. Ordinary people were hardly mentioned in the terms.

On his way home from the Third Crusade, Richard I was captured in Austria, and money was raised in English taxes to pay his ransom. When Richard died fighting in France in 1199, his brother, John, became king. John was outwitted by the French king, Philip, so that by 1204 most of the English lands in France had been lost. In 1215, the English barons made John sign Magna Carta, which set down their feudal rights. But a war between the king and the barons soon followed.

When John died in 1216, his 9-year-old son became king as Henry III. Until he was 20, the king's counsellors ruled England in his name. Henry spent money on palaces, castles, and on rebuilding Westminster Abbey. He chose French friends and advisors, which further annoyed the barons. In 1258 they demanded that he should consult them regularly at meetings of the Great Council. Leading the barons was Simon de Montfort, the king's French brother-in-law. His army fought the king's forces at Lewes in Sussex in 1264 and took Henry and his warrior son, Edward, prisoners.

▷ **The king needed to collect taxes to pay for his army.** By 1130, money, not goods, was the usual way to pay rent.
● To add up money quickly, counters and coins were moved around a squared (chequered) tablecloth, as shown here.
● "Exchequers" were appointed to collect and manage the spending of the money.
● Sheriffs were in charge of local exchequers.

▷ **The Parliament, or Council, of Edward I, in 1274.** On the king's left is Llywelyn of Wales; on his right, Alexander III of Scotland. Also present are the archbishops of Canterbury and York. On woolsacks in the middle sit the Chancellor, the chief minister, and judges. Today the Lord Chancellor still sits on a woolsack in the House of Lords.

In 1265 de Montfort called a Council, or Parliament. For the first time, spokesmen from both towns and country shires met with the nobles. It was a step towards today's Parliament of lords and "commons".

But soon after, Prince Edward escaped and roused support for his father among barons afraid of de Montfort's power. At Evesham in 1265 de Montfort was killed in battle and Henry regained his crown. Edward then went on Crusade. While returning in 1272, he learnt his father had died. Now king, Edward wanted the Council to grant him money for his wars. It did, and got more power in return.

◁ **Churchmen were usually the only officials who could read.** Some became Chancellor, originally the writer of royal letters.

THE CONQUEST OF WALES

The Normans had fought hard to subdue Wales. For 200 years, the Welsh fought fiercely to defend their mountainous land. But they also fought one another, and this was their undoing. Edward I of England brought Wales under English rule by 1300.

The Normans had taken over lowland Wales, but left the mountain kingdoms to the Welsh princes. Powerful barons on the English border fought off Welsh raids and took sides in the quarrels between Welsh princes. Strong rulers, such as Rhys ap Gruffudd (who died in 1197), fought for overall power, while the English tried to stop the Welsh uniting under one leader.

The strongest Welsh kingdom was Gwynedd. Llywelyn the Great, Prince of Gwynedd, conquered Snowdonia and Powys and, by his death in 1240, had won control of all Wales. His grandson, Llywelyn II, claimed the title of Prince of Wales in 1267, and this was recognized by Henry III of England.

▽ **Coronation of Edward I**. He was a strong ruler and fought successfully in Wales, Scotland and France. He ended Wales's independence.

◁ **The Welsh were admired as good soldiers.** Welsh archers fought in the English army. Their favourite weapon was the longbow, being used here.
● The bow was made of wood, usually yew.
● It was as tall as a man, and needed a pull of about 45 kg to draw it.
● An archer could shoot an arrow about 180 metres, firing six shots a minute.

▷ **The death of Llywelyn the Great,** mourned by his sons. Welsh culture, art and literature continued to flourish after the English conquest.

▽ **English soldiers discuss work on the building of Conway Castle,** north Wales, by Edward I in about 1285. The castle still stands.

Llywelyn then angered the new English king, Edward I, by attacking border castles. In 1277 an English army invaded Wales, overran the south, and attacked Llywelyn's mountain strongholds. The Welsh made peace. Llywelyn kept most of his lands and his title. But in 1282 his brother, David, led a revolt which Llywelyn joined. Both were killed in battle by Edward's forces.

Wales now had an English king, but its lands were not made part of England. Edward split Llywelyn's lands into six new counties, where English law had to be obeyed. Large estates with English owners swallowed up the traditional small lands owned by Welsh nobles.

Edward founded new towns with English settlers to encourage crafts and trade. He built a chain of castles to guard north Wales. These huge castles, such as Harlech, Conway and Caernarvon, are among the most impressive buildings of medieval Britain.

In 1301 Edward gave his son Edward, born at Caernarvon, the title of Prince of Wales.

SCOTLAND AT WAR

England and Scotland were also uneasy neighbours in the Middle Ages. England was the larger and stronger country. Scotland's mix of peoples did not think of themselves as a nation until the 13th century. A series of wars against England were costly for both countries, but victory helped to unite the Scots.

▷ **Bannockburn made Robert the Bruce** a Scottish national hero.
● The battle was fought near Stirling Castle, held by the English.
● The Scots were out-numbered three to one, but the English cavalry became stuck in a marsh.
● Unable to move freely, they were hacked down by Scots foot-soldiers.
● The English army fled.

▽ **Edward I's coronation chair** in Westminster Abbey enclosed the Stone of Scone on which Scottish kings were crowned. It was returned to Scotland in 1996.

English kings often tried to control and force laws on Scottish kings. And when there was no clear heir to the Scottish throne, trouble was likely.

Alexander III was the last Scottish king in direct line from Malcolm Canmore. He died in 1286, leaving as heir his 3-year-old granddaughter, Margaret. The Scots nobles decided she should marry Edward I of England, but she died in 1290. As the Scots could not decide on a new king, they asked Edward for help. He chose a noble, John Balliol, thinking that Balliol would do what he was told. But Balliol rebelled, and asked France for help. Edward invaded Scotland with a small army in 1296, forcing Balliol to give up the crown.

△ **Edward III (right) and David II of Scotland** make peace in 1357. Edward had repeatedly beaten the Scots in battle.

Battles for Scotland

N

SCOTLAND

Bannockburn ✕

Glasgow ✕

Stirling Bridge

Edward's campaigns
← 1296
← 1298
← 1300
← 1301
← 1303

Falkirk

ENGLAND

△ **Edward I's battles to take Scotland,** from 1296 to 1303.

Sir William Wallace (about 1272–1305) was not of high enough rank to claim the crown. He became "guardian" of Scotland.

● Defeated by Edward I's archers and knights at Falkirk in 1298, he fled abroad to seek aid.

● In 1303 he took up the fight again. The English defeated his forces at Glasgow in 1305.

Edward tried to govern Scotland himself. But William Wallace led the Scots in revolt, beating the English at Stirling Bridge in 1297. Then he was captured and executed in London in 1305. A new leader, Robert the Bruce, gained the backing of Scots nobles and had himself crowned king in 1306.

In 1307 Edward I of England died while preparing to lead his army for the sixth time into Scotland. His son, Edward II, was no soldier, and faced unrest in England, made worse by the cost of the Scottish wars. Led by Bruce, the Scots seized their chance. At the start of the Battle of Bannockburn in 1314, Bruce killed an English knight in single combat, inspiring his men to victory.

In 1328, a new English king, the young Edward III, agreed to respect Scotland's independence. This did not stop him attacking four years later and capturing Bruce's son, King David II, for ransom. But the Scottish monarchy survived. David's successor was Robert II, the first of a new royal line called the Stuarts.

TRADE AND INDUSTRY

In medieval Britain there were no factories, and few merchant ships for trading abroad. Wealth came from the land, and from selling what the land produced – especially wool (and later woollen cloth) which people wove by hand at home.

Wool was England's most valuable product, carried by packhorses to ports such as Southampton and Ipswich. From there, sailing ships called cogs took it to the clothmakers of Flanders. Leather and corn were also sold abroad, and coal was shipped from the north-east to London. A rich person paid for a trading voyage, in return for a share in any profit. The Church disapproved. Its view was that a man could profit only from his own labour and not by investing in a business he took no part in. Nevertheless, trade grew, mainly with Europe.

There was a rising demand for luxuries. In England, the town of Malvern supplied tiles; Lincoln, scarlet cloth; Norwich, a coarser material for tapestries; and Winchester, bed covers.

▽ **Industries of medieval Britain included:**
● Wool from sheep (below) and later cloth
● leather
● tin mining in Cornwall
● lead mining in Yorkshire and Somerset
● salt mining in Cheshire.

▷ **Ships trading with Britain** carried:
● wine from Gascony in France
● wax and canvas from the Holy Roman Empire
● furs from the Baltic
● cloth and lace from Flanders (north-east France and Belgium)
● rugs, sugar cane, figs, raisins, and spices from the East, first brought back by Crusaders.

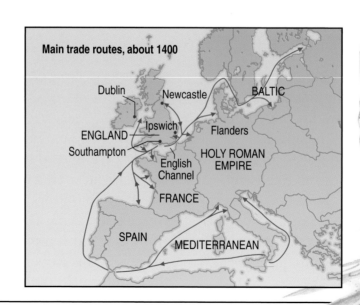

Main trade routes, about 1400

Dublin
Newcastle
BALTIC
Ipswich
ENGLAND
Flanders
Southampton
HOLY ROMAN EMPIRE
English Channel
FRANCE
SPAIN
MEDITERRANEAN

By 1300 England had more than 15 million sheep. The large Cotswold "wool churches" show how prosperous wool villages became. People made their own cloth, and a spinning wheel and loom stood in most houses. Woollen cloth gradually took over from raw wool as England's chief export. New towns such as Leeds and Bradford grew around the cloth industry, which needed flowing streams to drive the watermills of the fullers (who cleaned the wool).

△ **Lavenham Church, Suffolk,** built in the 1480s by local people with money gained from the local wool industry.

◁ **Merchants oversee the loading and unloading of goods** at a harbour on the south coast of England. The import and export trade created jobs for dockers, shipbuilders, carpenters, weavers, dyers, miners.

TOWNS AND HOUSES

Towns grew with trade. They were busy with carts and horses, noisy with the cries of pedlars, beggars, and shopkeepers, and dirty with rubbish. Most houses were small, but a wealthy merchant could afford a large two-storey house and furniture.

Houses were squashed together in the narrow streets of medieval towns. Most homes were made of wood, with plastered walls, but stone was also used. At a merchant's house, the second floor jutted out over the street, and there was often a back yard or garden. On the ground floor was a large hall, where the family ate and entertained guests. Upstairs were the solar, a parlour (for private business) and bedrooms, with an attic for the servants.

The kitchen was sometimes in the yard (to reduce the risk of fire). Water was fetched from a river or well, or bought from street-sellers. There was no bathroom; people went to the public bathhouse, and most used outside toilets. Indoor toilets emptied through the wall or into a cesspit in the cellar.

▷ **A wealthy family's house within a town.** By the 13th century, rich people had much furniture and slept in wooden beds, with linen sheets. Glass windows became fashionable for the rich in the 1300s.

◁ **Thirteenth-century kitchen pots.**

Town life
People got up at daybreak. A bell was rung when the town gates were opened, and the day's business began.
● Streets were muddy and smelly because people threw rubbish into the open drains.
● Chickens, pigs, and cows were kept in yards next to houses.
● At night the curfew bell rang. People put out their fires, closed the shutters over windows, barred their doors, and went to bed.

◁ **The ruins of a medieval peasant's house** in Scotland, in which a family lived.

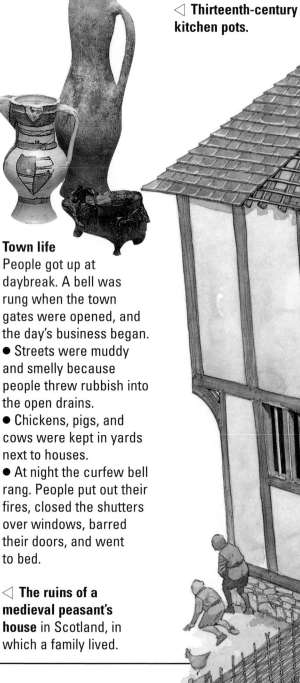

Few houses had ovens.
Most food was boiled, or roasted on a spit. Women or servants often took ingredients to the local baker or pie-maker to make pies and pastries. Other favourites were eels, cod, herring, ham, fruit, cheese. Meat and fish were salted or dried to preserve them. Garden herbs and spices were used in cooking. Crusaders first brought pepper, cloves, and sugar (a rarity) from the East.

31

GUILDS AND CRAFTS

By 1400 merchants and craftworkers were growing more important. Each trade guarded its skills by forming groups called guilds, which came to control town affairs. Guild members built churches, made clothes and furniture, sold meat and fish in the markets, and fashioned jewellery from gold.

△ **Tanners making leather.** They cleaned and soaked animal skins in a mixture of water and chemicals from plants. It was dirty, smelly work. Workshops often gave a street its name, for example, Tanner Lane. So, too, did items for sale, such as Bread Street, Fish Alley. Many of these names exist to this day.

Guilds were set up by townspeople, and at first included people from all trades. Once a town had the right to form a guild, granted by royal charter, only guild members were allowed to trade there. Later, trades formed their own guilds. There were guilds of skinners, fishmongers, tailors, tanners, painters, and so on. Although not full guild members, women were active in some trades, especially clothing, baking, and embroidery. A widow often carried on her dead husband's business.

△ **A 15th-century ring** bearing a tradesman's mark.

▽ **Tapestries were embroidered** and hung on walls in rich people's houses. Painters decorated the walls of churches (right).

▷ **Craftsmen add the finishing touches** to the new tower of Ely Cathedral. The old tower fell down in 1322, and was soon replaced.

▽ **A medieval stained glass window,** made by a glazier, shows a farmer sowing seeds.

◁ **A stonemason demonstrates his work** to his guild leader. Guilds taught their crafts to boy apprentices.
● Apprentices lived with a master-craftsman.
● Their training lasted up to 7 years.
● After training, the apprentice became a "journeyman". A master paid him wages.
● To become a guild member, he had to produce a masterpiece – a test piece to show his workmanship was good.

The guilds set business standards by fixing prices, weights, and measures. A guild also set standards of work. It could fine or expel a member whose work fell below standard. Guilds organized religious processions, paid for schools, and produced entertainments, such as yearly pageants. From the guilds grew London's livery companies, whose members were all rich merchants, rather than ordinary craftsmen.

Building workers were busy in the 14th and 15th centuries, constructing some of Britain's finest medieval buildings. These included the cathedral at Exeter (finished about 1360), the guildhall at King's Lynn, and colleges at Oxford and Cambridge. Such projects involved many trades: stone masons, carpenters, plasterers, glaziers (glass-workers), and plumbers (who put the lead on the roof). One of the masterpieces of medieval building was the hammer-beam roof of Westminster Hall. Commissioned by Richard II, it was completed around 1400.

MARKETS AND FAIRS

To a medieval fair came "all manner of men, the mean (poor) and the rich", wrote William Langland in 1370. Most villages and towns held weekly markets, where people sold their goods. Fairs, held once or twice a year, gave people the chance to enjoy themselves.

Any peasant could take vegetables or cheese to sell at the town market, though he had to pay a tax to stand in the square with his goods spread out on the floor. Richer traders set up stalls. Fairs were international markets. Merchants came to the great fair at Stourbridge near Cambridge from as far away as Germany and Italy. Norwich and London also had big fairs. A fair might last 3 weeks, filling the town with traders, travellers, pedlars, doctors, fortune-tellers, and entertainers. Kings encouraged fairs because they brought in money from abroad. William I started St Giles' Fair in Winchester, but later the local bishop took charge of it, and collected the taxes.

△ **Rich and poor people went** to the fair to see minstrels, jugglers, fire-eaters, sword-swallowers, acrobats, buffoons (clowns), and musicians.

Food-sellers sold pies, beer, and nuts. Herring pie was a favourite snack. People gambled on cockfights, wrestlers, and dogs baiting (fighting) bears.

△ **Part of a medieval manuscript** showing an old French song like those sung by minstrels to entertain crowds at fairs. The manuscript is illustrated with knights dressed to look like animals for a pantomime.

△ **Market day** was a chance for people to meet old friends, gossip and do business. Crowds jostled around the stalls, and laughed and jeered at actors and entertainers.

● Merchants, known as cheapmen, set up stalls in churchyards, until this was banned in 1285.

● People could buy vegetables, live animals, pots, pans, and knives.

● Anyone who broke market rules was punished by the market court, meeting in a hut known as the Tolbooth.

● Pickpockets and thieves risked a stay in the town gaol (jail).

▷ **This misericord** (on which monks rested in church) shows two thieves. Markets and fairs attracted criminals.

Entertainment was part of the fun of the fair. For country villagers, especially children, it was a treat to watch an acrobat or a stilt-walker. But not everyone liked the entertainers. The poet Langland wrote that "if it were not for their dirty jokes, no one would give them so much as a farthing (a small coin worth a quarter of a penny)".

There were no theatres, but plays were performed in churches or on carts. Medieval plays were religious. The early ones were given by town guilds who performed miracle plays, acting out stories from the Bible and the lives of the saints. In the morality plays of the 1400s, actors staged tales of good versus evil. Everyman (the ordinary person) had to choose between Vice (the Devil) and Virtue (goodness).

THE BLACK DEATH

In 1348 a terrible disease struck Britain. It was called the Black Death. The same plague had killed millions of people as it swept across Asia and the Continent. Doctors could do little for those who fell ill, and so many died that some villages were left empty. About a third of England's four million people died.

The plague came from the East and travelled with horrifying speed. It was carried by fleas on diseased black rats. Rats travelled on ships, and the plague spread from port to port. The Black Death was in Italy in January 1348. It reached England in the summer, probably at a Dorset port, and by November it was in London. People fled the city in panic and so spread the disease further. By 1349 it had reached Wales, Ireland, and Scotland.

"Fruitful country places were abandoned", wrote the Bishop of Winchester. Church records show how parish priests died and were replaced, until no more could be found. Scientists then did not know the real cause of the plague. They blamed "corrupt air" or the movement of the planets for the outbreak. Some people saw the Black Death as a sign of God's anger. Doctors, beggars, seamen and travellers were shunned as carriers of the disease. The only defence was to flee.

After the terrible years of 1348 and 1349, the "pestilence" came back several times before the 1400s. The Black Death caused huge loss of life and confusion in towns and country-side – yet Britain recovered with surprising speed.

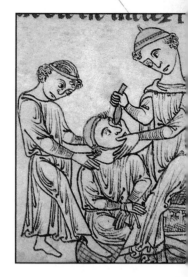

▷ **Doctors and other healers tried many remedies for diseases,** like herbal medicines for eye infections, as here.

In the Middle Ages, people mainly died through poor hygiene, dirty water supplies, or common diseases. Monks and nuns treated the sick, and operations were performed by barbers or travelling "quack" (pretend) doctors. They could sew up wounds and make medicines, but theirs was a dangerous job. A failed operation on a lord could end with the surgeon's execution!

▷ **The Black Death killed most people who caught it.** Some had egg-sized boils on their bodies, and fever. Others coughed blood. Some people went to bed well and were dead by morning. They were buried in mass graves (right). Doctors were powerless to help. As precautions, they told people to:
● cover windows
● avoid sleeping on their backs.
● breathe in toilet smells!

▷ **Parents mourn a young victim of the Black Death.** A priest comforts the parents.
● In the street, dead people are being carried from a house, which has been marked as unclean with a red death cross.
● A religious procession passes by, with nuns praying to God to stop his anger.

REVOLT AND REBELLION

"This world is but a highway full of woe, and we are pilgrims, passing to and fro", wrote Chaucer in his *Canterbury Tales*. For England, the 14th century ended in strife. There was a peasants' revolt, conflict between king and nobles, and an uprising in Wales.

Edward III of England reigned for 50 years. By the 1370s he was old and feeble. His soldier son, the Black Prince, died in 1376. When the old king died a year later, his 10-year-old grandson became King Richard II. The boy's uncle, John of Gaunt, ruled for him.

Richard's kingdom was restless. Outbreaks of the plague lasted into the 1370s, but people who survived had the chance of a better way of life. As prices fell and wages rose, some peasants could afford a stone house for the first time.

Richard was artistic, and encouraged court writers such as Chaucer, whose lively characters seem hopeful on the whole. But they also complained about priests and the Church.

Many people called for reforms in the Church, including the Oxford scholar John Wycliffe and his followers, called Lollards. Most Lollards were poor people. They questioned the amounts of money spent on churches, and some of the Church's teachings such as the devotion to saints' bones and other holy relics. Nobles and bishops feared a similar attack on their wealth and property, and so persecuted the Lollards. Wycliffe escaped being burned at the stake, but around 1405 many Lollards were put to death in this cruel way.

△ **Peasants rampage in London in 1381.** Like-minded Londoners let the protesters into the city. The mob burned the homes of officials and attacked the Tower of London, where nobles were hiding.

England had lost money and land in its wars with both Scotland and France. Parliament blamed the king's ministers for the disasters. When the ministers raised taxes to cover the cost, many people refused to pay. In 1381, such discontent led to the Peasants' Revolt. The worst riots were in Essex and Kent, led by Wat Tyler and the priest John Ball. Many nobles were attacked or killed.

◁ **Richard II's meeting with the rebels** during the Peasants' Revolt. He did not keep promises to ease their grievances.
● Richard spoke with the forces of the rebel leader, Wat Tyler, outside London's walls, as shown on the right of this painting. The king agreed to Tyler's demands.
● But during the peace talks, Tyler was wounded, as shown on the left.
● Richard cried to the angry mob, "Sirs, will you shoot your king?" The peasants went away without the reforms they wanted.

◁ **Owen Glendower** led a Welsh revolt against Henry IV. This was Glendower's Parliament House in Powys.
● The revolt began in north Wales in 1400, and quickly spread.
● At Shrewsbury in 1405, the king's army defeated the Welsh.
● By 1410, the revolt was over. Glendower became a fugitive, and died about 1416.

△ **The Peasants' Revolt** of 1381 was caused by anger at raised taxes and a freeze on wage rises.
● Peasants had no voice in Parliament and sought justice from the king.
● A peasant army from south and east England marched into London.
● Its leaders were Wat Tyler and John Ball.
● Travelling preachers like Ball blamed the Church and nobles for greed and corruption.
● Ball was hanged.

Richard's bravery helped to end the revolt, but his choice of pleasure-loving friends upset his advisors. The friends were removed by Parliament. In 1397 Richard took revenge. He seized John of Gaunt's estates and sent his cousin, Henry Bolingbroke, into exile. Richard scorned Parliament, and more nobles feared losing their lands. When Bolingbroke came back to England, many joined him, and in 1399 he took the crown as Henry IV. Richard was kept prisoner until he died in 1400, probably murdered. To keep firm hold on the throne, the new king made sure his own son, Henry V, was crowned in 1413.

THE HUNDRED YEARS' WAR

Since 1066, kings of England had ruled lands in France. In 1337 Edward III of England claimed the right to rule all France. So began the series of wars known as the Hundred Years' War. They lasted until 1453. The English won most of the battles. But when the wars ended, England held only a tiny part of France.

△ **Mons Meg** – a siege gun used in civil wars in Scotland in the 1450s. The cannon trolley is a copy of one built in the 1480s.

Edward claimed the French throne because his mother, Isabella, was the daughter of King Philip "the Fair" of France. The English king was a good general. His army won a sea battle at Sluys in 1340, and the land battles of Crécy in 1346 and Poitiers in 1356. However, neither Edward nor his son, the Black Prince, managed to conquer France.

While Richard II was king, there was a short peace. But fighting began again in the 1400s when Henry V claimed France. The French had a mad king and were split by quarrels. War gave Henry the chance to unite England and France. He took an army across the Channel and marched through France. Although his soldiers were weak with disease and outnumbered, Henry led them to victory at Agincourt in 1415.

△ **Cannon** were used at the Battle of Crécy in 1346. Henry V had 75 gunners, who bombarded French towns.

△ **With the soldiers** went armourers, grooms, priests, surgeons, and smiths. Women joined as helpers.

△ **Some bowmen used crossbows too.** These were drawn by winding a handle, and could shoot arrows through armour.

△ **A squire** looked after a knight's armour, which packhorses carried. The squire helped the knight dress for battle.

△ **Siege of a French town.** The English fired cannon to smash down the walls. Both sides suffered from disease when sieges dragged on. After the town's capture or surrender, the victorious soldiers usually plundered the town, as here, with the best treasure going to the king.

War in the 15th century was brutal. Both sides held knights for ransom, but killed poor prisoners. Townspeople were driven from besieged towns by their own soldiers. Armies on the march robbed, stole food, and burned villages.

By 1420 Henry was master of France. He married the French king's daughter, and was named heir to the French throne. But in 1422 he died, leaving a baby son, also called Henry. A council of nobles took charge until the young king could rule for himself. Meanwhile, Joan of Arc roused the French to fight the English. She was caught and burned to death, but France triumphed. By 1455 Henry VI held only Calais.

△ **Foot soldiers** wore everyday clothes. English soldiers carried stakes to Agincourt for barricades, as well as weapons.

△ **English archers** had longbows, which they carried wrapped in cloth. They wore leather jerkins, and carried food in sacks.

△ **A knight** wore steel armour, as did his horse. He carried a shield and used an axe or mace to fight hand-to-hand.

△ **Pages** served the knights. At Agincourt, many pages were killed while helping knights unhorse in boggy ground.

THE WARS OF THE ROSES

From the 1450s until 1485, there was war again in England. Two families fought for the throne in battles between nobles. Ordinary people knew or cared little about it, and there were long periods of peace in which the country prospered. In the end, England was united by a noble from a third family, the Tudors.

Britain was clearly changing. Peasants could buy farms and so become small landowners, called yeomen. English, not French, was the language of officials in government. Universities flourished and trade grew, with woollen cloth as England's most valuable export. Owning money was becoming more important than owning land.

Yet a rebellion by yeomen and knights in 1450 showed there was discontent. Henry VI suffered bouts of madness, and most of his duties were performed by his wife, Margaret of Anjou. Nobles with private armies, like the Earl of Warwick and Richard, Duke of York, had real control of much of England.

Richard of York's claim to the crown was at least as good as Henry VI's. His supporters, the Yorkists, took a white rose as their badge. The Lancastrians – Henry's men – wore a red rose. After the Duke of York was killed in 1460, his son won the battle of Towton and made himself king, as Edward IV. Queen Margaret schemed for Henry's return, and he was briefly restored in 1470. But then Edward IV won the battles of Barnet and Tewkesbury. He captured the queen and killed her son. Henry VI ended his days in the Tower of London.

Edward IV kept taxes low and encouraged trade. At his death in 1483, he left a 12-year-old son, Edward V, and an ambitious brother, Richard of Gloucester.

▷ **Henry Tudor becomes King Henry VII** after winning the Battle of Bosworth. Legend has it that Sir William Stanley, who deserted Richard, picked up the crown from under a bush on the battlefield and gave it to Henry. Henry VII traced his family back to Edward III.

△ **Portrait of Edward IV,** who reigned near the end of the medieval period. By this time, many people could read and write English. In 1476, William Caxton set up the first printing press in England.

Edward and his younger brother were taken to the Tower, never to be free again. Richard made himself king. He ruled well, but few people trusted him. They believed he had ordered his nephews' deaths.

Another noble now challenged for the crown. Henry Tudor, a Lancastrian exiled in France, landed in Wales. By defeating Richard at Bosworth, Henry VII won the crown. By marrying Edward IV's daughter, Elizabeth, he united the sides that had fought the "Wars of the Roses". The Tudor Age had begun.

△▷ **In August 1485 Henry Tudor fought Richard III at Bosworth in Leicestershire.** Richard was let down by supporters who changed sides. He was killed on the battlefield, which is now marked by a well where Richard drank, below.

Wars of the Roses (major battles)

N

Towton ✕

Bosworth ✕

Tewkesbury ✕   St Albans ✕

Barnet ✕

FAMOUS PEOPLE OF MEDIEVAL BRITAIN

Anselm (about 1033–1109) was Archbishop of Canterbury from 1093.

Roger Bacon (about 1220–92) was a Franciscan friar and scientist. He was accused by his enemies of being a magician.

Thomas Becket (1118–70) was Chancellor of England and Archbishop of Canterbury. He quarrelled with Henry II and was murdered (see page 19).

Robert the Bruce (1274–1329) was king of Scotland. His victory at Bannockburn preserved Scotland's independence from England (see page 26).

William Caxton (about 1422–about 1491) was the first English printer. He learned his trade in Germany, and set up a printing press at Westminster in 1476.

Geoffrey Chaucer (about 1341–1400) was the greatest writer of medieval Britain. He wrote the unfinished *Canterbury Tales,* in English (see pages 5, 38).

Geoffrey Chaucer

Edward III (1312–77) was the English king who began the Hundred Years' War with France. His son was Edward,

the Black Prince (1330–76).

Eleanor of Aquitaine (about 1122–1204) was the wife of Henry II of England. She was first married to the future king of France. By marrying Henry, she brought her French lands into English control.

Owen Glendower or Glyndwr (about 1359–1416) led the last great Welsh rebellion against England (see page 39).

John Gower (about 1330–1408) was an English poet, and a friend of Geoffrey Chaucer.

Hereward the Wake (alive 1070) led an English rebellion against the Normans, and became the hero of many stories.

Joan of Arc (1412–31) led French resistance to English conquest. She was burned at the stake and later made a saint.

John of Gaunt, Duke of Lancaster (1340–99) was the fourth son of Edward III. He tried to become king of Spain. His son became Henry IV, and he was also the ancestor of Henry VII, the first of the Tudors.

Lanfranc (about 1005–89) Italian-born, was William the Conqueror's advisor and Archbishop of Canterbury from 1070 (see page 19).

William Langland (about 1332–1400) was an English poet, who wrote The *Vision of Piers Plowman.*

Stephen Langton (about 1155–1228) was Archbishop of Canterbury and supported the barons in their struggles against King John.

Llywelyn ap Gruffud (died 1282) was the last Welsh prince of Wales; he was defeated by Edward I of England.

Malcolm III Canmore (about 1031–93) was king of Scotland. He was killed fighting the English. His descendants ruled Scotland until 1290 (see page 26).

Margaret of Anjou (1430–82) married Henry VI of England in 1455. Her son and husband were killed by the Yorkists during the Wars of the Roses. She died in France (see page 42).

Matilda (1102–67) was Henry I's daughter. She was not accepted as England's ruler, and waged war against her cousin Stephen of Blois (1097–1154). Her son was Henry II (see page 13).

Matilda

Simon de Montfort (about 1208–65) led the barons' revolt against Henry III (see page 22). He was killed at the Battle of Evesham.

Richard I, the Lionheart (1157–99) was England's famous crusading king. He fought in the Holy Land, was held for ransom in Austria, and died in France (see page 22).

Robin Hood (possibly late 1100s) was a legendary outlaw and opponent of King John. Many stories grew up about him, but no one knows if he was a real person.

Wat Tyler (died 1381) was a leader of the Peasants' Revolt (see page 39). He may have been an ex-soldier.

Richard Whittington (died 1423), now known as a pantomime hero, was a Gloucestershire cloth merchant who became very rich and was three times Lord Mayor of London.

Richard Whittington

John Wycliffe (about 1329–84) helped write a new English translation of the Bible and led the Lollard protest movement for Church reform (see page 38).

York, Duke of (Richard Plantagenet) (1411–60) led the Yorkist opposition to Henry VI (see page 42). He was killed in battle at Wakefield. His sons became Edward IV and Richard III.

MEDIEVAL ROYAL FAMILY TREE

This tree shows the main branches of the royal family of England during and following on from the Medieval monarchs.

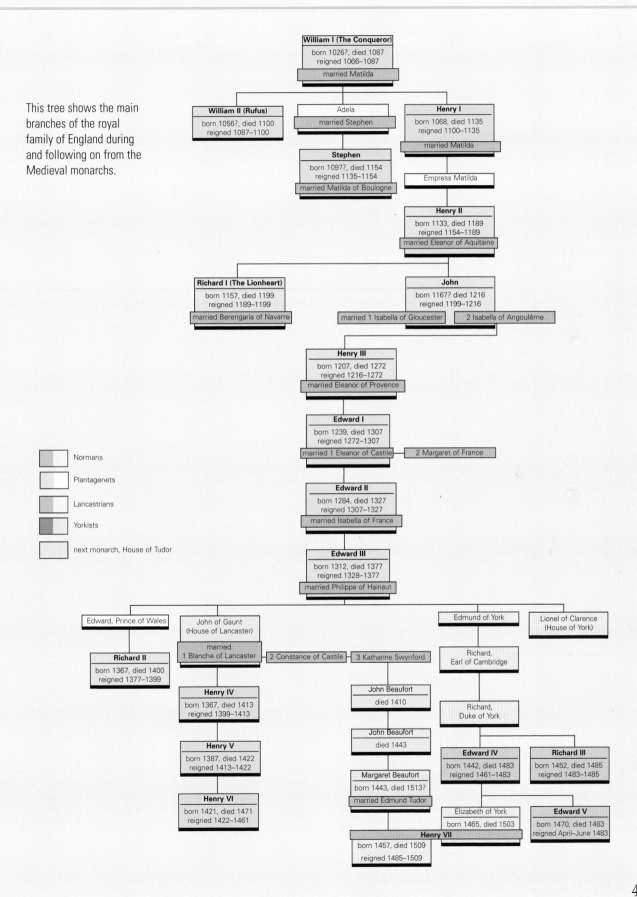

William I (The Conqueror)
born 1026?, died 1087
reigned 1066–1087
married Matilda

William II (Rufus)
born 1056?, died 1100
reigned 1087–1100

Adela
married Stephen

Henry I
born 1068, died 1135
reigned 1100–1135
married Matilda

Stephen
born 1097?, died 1154
reigned 1135–1154
married Matilda of Boulogne

Empress Matilda

Henry II
born 1133, died 1189
reigned 1154–1189
married Eleanor of Aquitaine

Richard I (The Lionheart)
born 1157, died 1199
reigned 1189–1199
married Berengaria of Navarre

John
born 1167? died 1216
reigned 1199–1216
married 1 Isabella of Gloucester   2 Isabella of Angoulême

Henry III
born 1207, died 1272
reigned 1216–1272
married Eleanor of Provence

Edward I
born 1239, died 1307
reigned 1272–1307
married 1 Eleanor of Castile   2 Margaret of France

Edward II
born 1284, died 1327
reigned 1307–1327
married Isabella of France

Edward III
born 1312, died 1377
reigned 1328–1377
married Philippa of Hainaut

Edward, Prince of Wales

John of Gaunt
(House of Lancaster)
married
1 Blanche of Lancaster   2 Constance of Castile   3 Katharine Swynford

Edmund of York

Lionel of Clarence
(House of York)

Richard II
born 1367, died 1400
reigned 1377–1399

Henry IV
born 1367, died 1413
reigned 1399–1413

John Beaufort
died 1410

Richard,
Earl of Cambridge

Henry V
born 1387, died 1422
reigned 1413–1422

John Beaufort
died 1443

Richard,
Duke of York

Henry VI
born 1421, died 1471
reigned 1422–1461

Margaret Beaufort
born 1443, died 1513?
married Edmund Tudor

Edward IV
born 1442, died 1483
reigned 1461–1483

Richard III
born 1452, died 1485
reigned 1483–1485

Elizabeth of York
born 1465, died 1503

Edward V
born 1470, died 1483
reigned April–June 1483

Henry VII
born 1457, died 1509
reigned 1485–1509

Normans

Plantagenets

Lancastrians

Yorkists

next monarch, House of Tudor

GLOSSARY

acre area of land equal to 4,047 square metres (about the area of a football pitch)

apprentice boy learning a craft

archbishop high official of the Church; England had two, based at Canterbury and York

archer soldier with bow and arrows

bailiff person who organizes work on the land

baron noble and landowner

bishop official of the Church, in charge of an area called a diocese

craftworkers people who earned their living by a skill or special trade, such as blacksmiths, potters, shoemakers

Crusades wars fought against Muslims by Christian armies from Europe for the Holy Land (Palestine)

embroidery making patterns and pictures with stitches on fabric

feudalism system of land-holding and government in western Europe during the Middle Ages. People held land from someone of higher rank, or social class, in return for service. The highest rank was the monarch (king or queen), the lowest rank the peasants.

fief land held in return for military service

government people who run the country: the monarch, Parliament and local officials such as sheriffs and exchequers

guild association of traders or craftworkers

hide area of land, enough to support a whole family

jury group of men that were present in a court of law to name suspects and hear evidence

keep central stronghold of a Norman castle

knight soldier on horseback; a man promoted to high rank by the king and sworn to do good deeds

land-holding living on land owned by someone else, usually to whom rent, goods, or unpaid work had to be given

livery uniform or clothes that show the wearer belongs to a guild or to an employer

loom frame used to weave cloth

lord powerful local ruler such as a knight or baron

manor estate, with manor house and fields

manuscript book or story written by hand

medieval to do with the Middle Ages

merchants people who made their living by buying and selling things, either in their own country or abroad

monastery buildings lived in by monks

monk man who lives in a monastery and is devoted to religious life

noble local ruler and landowner, also known as a lord

parliament nobles and important churchmen who advised the monarch on raising taxes and running the country

peasant person living from the land, farming a small area or plot

pilgrims people travelling to a religious centre or holy place. The journeys they make are called pilgrimages.

Pope head of the Catholic Christian Church in Rome

relics holy remains, such as saints' bones

saint especially holy person, honoured by the Church

seal engraved design, often on a ring, for stamping in hot wax as a person's identity mark on a document

serf peasant who was not a free man and owned no land

sheriff local official, responsible for overseeing a shire, which is a small area of the countryside with its own elected council

smith metalworker making tools and weapons of iron

steward manager of a lord's estate

stocks wooden frame, with holes for feet and sometimes hands and head, in which criminals were locked as punishment

taxes money collected by nobles and kings from the people to pay for buildings or to equip the army and navy

treaty agreement between two sides, for example, to end a war

vassal person who held land from the king or a lord, promising loyalty and military service

villein farmer whose land belonged to the lord of the manor

yeoman farmer who owns and works his own land

FIND OUT MORE

BOOKS

A Castle at War, Andrew Langley (Dorling Kindersley, 1998)

Danger Zone: Avoid Being a Prisoner in a Medieval Dungeon!, Fiona Macdonald (Book House, 2003)

Eyewitness: Medieval Life, Andrew Langley (Dorling Kindersley, 2004)

Medieval World: Manners and Customs in the Middle Ages, Marsha Groves (Crabtree, 2005)

Picture the Past: Life in a Medieval Castle, Jane Shuter (Heinemann Library, 2005)

The Best Book of Knights and Castles, Deborah Murrell (Kingfisher, 2005)

WEBSITES

www.britannia.com/history

This directory includes resources on medieval Britain.

www.camelotintl.com/village

Find out what daily life in a medieval village was like.

www.castles-of-britain.com

Projects, newsletters, and other features all about medieval castles.

www.themiddleages.net

This wide-ranging website covers everything from the Normans to the Black Death.

www.timeref.org

This website gives a comprehensive picture of medieval life.

PLACES

In museums all over Britain you can see objects from medieval times, such as coins, jewellery, tools, armour, and pottery. There are manor houses, town houses, churches, cathedrals and castles to explore. These are just a few places to visit:

Beaumaris, Wales   A castle built by Edward I.

Caernarvon, Wales   A castle founded in the 1290s.

Castle Hedingham, Essex   A Norman castle.

Durham, County Durham   The cathedral and castle.

Edinburgh   Castle with St Margaret's Chapel (11th century), cathedral, Holyrood Abbey, and museums.

Kilkenny, Ireland   Medieval houses and friary buildings.

London   Museum of London, Tower of London, City churches, Westminster Abbey, and Westminster Hall.

Rievaulx, Yorkshire   The remains of monastery.

Rochester, Kent   A Norman castle, with the tallest keep in England.

Salisbury, Wiltshire   Cathedral built between 1220 and 1258.

York, Yorkshire   Cathedral with huge chapter house, stained glass, statues of 15 kings, The Shambles (900-year-old streets), and the castle museum.

INDEX

48